THE 8 HABITS OF

SUCCESSFUL TEENS

Living Authentically and Empowered

THE **8 HABITS** OF SUCCESSFUL TEENS
Living Authentically and Empowered

IRENE S. ROTH

Halo
PUBLISHING
INTERNATIONAL

Halo

PUBLISHING INTERNATIONAL

Halo Publishing International
7550 W IH-10 #800, PMB 2069
San Antonio, TX 78229

First Edition, November 2025
ISBN: 978-1-63765-857-4
Library of Congress Control Number: On File

Halo Publishing International is a self-publishing company that publishes adult fiction and non-fiction, children's literature, self-help, spiritual, and faith-based books. We continually strive to help authors reach their publishing goals and provide many different services that help them do so. We do not publish books that are deemed to be politically, religiously, or socially disrespectful, or books that are sexually provocative, including erotica. Halo reserves the right to refuse publication of any manuscript if it is deemed not to be in line with our principles. Do you have a book idea you would like us to consider publishing? Please visit www.halopublishing.com for more information.

To my parents, who empowered me
to be an authentic teen.

CONTENTS

PREFACE

Choosing Values in a Hyper-Connected World

*A*s I write this book, I can't ignore the reality that teenagers today face enormous challenges when it comes to living healthy, balanced lives—emotionally, mentally, and physically. One of the main reasons for this is that all of us, teens and adults alike, are constantly connected to our devices. Our phones are always within reach, buzzing with notifications, demanding our attention, and filling every spare moment with noise. I believe this constant connection is a serious challenge to our autonomy. It can be hard to live an excellent life when we're tethered to our devices eight or nine hours a day, allowing them to shape how we think, feel, and spend our time.

Not long ago, hyper-connectivity was seen as a "teen problem." Adults shook their heads at how much time teens spent texting or scrolling. But now I notice that more parents are just as connected—sometimes even more than their kids. Phones are usually present at the dinner table, during family outings, and even in quiet moments that used to invite conversation. How can kids learn healthy tech habits if they watch adults answering work emails during family time or scrolling through social media feeds instead of engaging with them? If we want teens to live with focus, purpose, and integrity, we as adults must first model that way of life.

So what does the over-consumption of technology have to do with the eight habits every teen needs to know to have a successful and meaningful life? In a word, everything. When we are always connected and distracted, we cannot focus on higher ambitions and purposes. Our attention becomes fragmented. We struggle to think clearly or pursue meaningful goals because we waste most of our time connected to our devices. Over time, we may even lose touch with who we are and what we really want out of life. This is why developing these eight habits of success is so crucial for teens. I really wish I had a book like this when I was growing up.

By clarifying what we truly believe and value, we create a personal compass that helps us navigate life's challenges with integrity and purpose. Without this clarity, it can be easy for us to be swayed by external pressures, constant notifications, and the endless noise of technology. Also, social media, news feeds, and digital distractions can subtly reshape what we think is important, pulling us toward comparison, outrage, or trends that don't even remotely align with who we really are. Knowing our core values allows us to make intentional choices instead of reacting impulsively or acting on autopilot.

This process of self-discovery takes time and reflection, but it is worth the effort. You might begin by asking yourself: What principles am I unwilling to compromise, no matter what the online world is saying? When have I felt most fulfilled, unplugged from technology? What matters to me so deeply that I would stand up for it, even if it made me unpopular? The answers to these questions will reveal patterns that underscore your deepest beliefs and values.

Once we know what we value, we can strive to live in alignment with those values. This is where our transformation starts. Our personal values become the filter through which we make decisions about how to spend our time, what opportunities to pursue, and even what kind of people we want to become. Without them, we are like a boat without a rudder, pushed around by whatever the culture, media, or our peers say is urgent.

Technology itself is not the enemy. Instead, it is a powerful tool that can enrich our lives when used wisely. It allows us to connect, learn, create, and share ideas in ways that previous generations could not imagine. However, when we let it dominate our lives, it can quickly rob us of the very things that make life meaningful: deep relationships, reflection, creativity, and inner peace, to name a few. The challenge, then, is to mindfully use technology rather than allowing it to use us.

Parents and mentors play a critical role in this process. Teens are watching us closely, often more closely than we think. They notice whether we put our phones down at dinner, whether we listen fully when they're talking to us, and whether we choose to spend time on things that really matter. Equally important, when they witness us living out our values, even in small daily ways, they're more likely to do the same.

The eight habits discussed in this book will build on this foundation. In the process, you'll learn how to focus your mind, make wise decisions, set meaningful goals, and take consistent action toward becoming your most authentic self. It is the key to living a successful life, no matter what challenges come our way. Before we begin, however, I'd like to pause to situate this book more concretely.

INTRODUCTION

If you're a teen reading this, I'm so glad you decided to come along on this journey. You've taken the first step toward building emotional well-being during what can be some of the most confusing and tumultuous years of your life.

Many of the habits our culture proposes that we develop in our teenage years can actually contribute to making us feel emptier and less fulfilled. Our technological culture keeps us distracted, reactive, and disconnected from ourselves. To grow into emotionally intelligent, confident, and authentic young adults, we need to pause, unplug, and make time for reflection and awareness on a regular basis.

Over the years, I've seen so many teens who feel unhappy, hopeless, or apathetic about life. Rates of depression and teen suicide are rising at alarming rates, and this breaks my heart. Your teen years should be filled with growth, discovery, and joy, not despair.

The good news is you have the power to change this. You can get into the driver's seat of your life. You can build a life filled with happiness, contentment, and peace. You can wake up with hope and purpose every day, succeed at what matters to you, and become your very best self. All it takes is learning new habits and changing a few negative mindsets. This book will guide you step-by-step in how to develop the healthy habits you need to live an emotionally strong, successful, and fulfilled life.

No matter where you come from, what your background is, or whether you are male or female, this book is for you, because every teen struggles to assert who they truly are during these years. You are not alone.

Over the years, as a teacher and youth mentor, I've heard many teens share their struggles. Here are a few random examples:

- "I want to succeed, but when I try, my friends call me a teacher's pet."
- "My parents are divorced, and I feel like I don't belong anywhere."
- "My mom always criticizes me. I feel worthless."
- "My parents tell me not to aim high, but I want more out of life."
- "My dad compares me to my brother. I'll never be good enough."
- "My parents fight constantly. I don't even feel safe at home."
- "I'm depressed and wish I knew how to feel better."
- "I do whatever my friends do—drink, take drugs, and engage in casual sex. I just don't know who I am anymore."

- "I feel that my life is out of control, and I hate myself."
- "My friends are all underachievers. How do I avoid following them?"

These struggles are real. You don't have to ignore them or face them alone. Instead, you can build tools and new, stronger mindsets to deal with them and create a better future for yourself.

The eight habits discussed in this book might seem simple, but they are difficult to appropriate into our lives. This process requires patience, commitment, and a willingness to grow.

One helpful way to understand these habits is to look at their opposites, i.e., the habits of unsuccessful teens. When you recognize what doesn't work, it can become easier to focus on what does. By practicing these eight habits, you'll develop your autonomy so you can live a successful, meaningful, and authentic life.

The eight habits are as follows:

Habit #1: Be Proactive

Take responsibility for your choices; act from intention rather than reaction.

Habit #2: Constantly Renew and Evolve

Embrace growth; learn from mistakes; leave behind what no longer serves you.

Habit #3: Be a Go-Getter

Take initiative and act on your goals; small, consistent actions build momentum.

Habit #4: Determine Your Beliefs and Values

Clarify what matters most; identify personal principles to guide decisions.

Habit #5: Develop Your Autonomy Through Boundaries

Protect your energy; make decisions aligned with your values; practice self-respect.

Habit #6: Be Your Best

Strive for excellence in daily actions; cultivate personal discipline and integrity.

Habit #7: Be Authentic

Express your true self; speak your truth; reject the need for external approval.

Habit #8: Live Authentically and Build Self-Esteem

Trust your inner voice; make choices that reflect your values; nurture self-worth and confidence.

Here's a clear breakdown of the **opposites** of each of the eight habits above—essentially, what it looks like when someone does the opposite of living autonomously.

Habit #1: Be Proactive → Be Reactive

Blame others or circumstances for what happens in your life. Wait for things to happen instead of taking initiative. Let emotions, impulses, and outside forces dictate your actions.

Habit #2: Constantly Renew and Evolve → Stay Stagnant

Avoid change and growth. Keep repeating the same patterns even when they don't work. Resist learning from mistakes and cling to what is comfortable, even if it holds you back.

Habit #3: Be a Go-Getter → Be Passive

Wait for opportunities to come to you instead of creating them. Avoid setting or pursuing goals. Allow fear, procrastination, or lack of motivation to prevent progress.

Habit #4: Determine Your Beliefs and Values → Drift Without Principles

Live by default, letting other people or society decide what matters. Make decisions based on trends, peer pressure, or convenience instead of core principles.

Habit #5: Develop Autonomy Through Boundaries → Have Weak or No Boundaries

Let others control your time, energy, and choices. Say yes when you mean no. Sacrifice your needs and values to please others or avoid conflict.

Habit #6: Be Your Best → Settle for Mediocrity

Do just enough to get by. Avoid challenges or personal discipline. Ignore opportunities to grow in character, skill, or integrity.

Habit #7: Be Authentic → Wear a Mask

Hide your true self to gain approval. Say what others want to hear, even if it goes against what you believe. Prioritize fitting in over living truthfully.

Habit #8: Live Authentically and Build Self-Esteem → Live Inauthentically and Undermine Yourself

Distrust your inner voice. Make choices that go against your values. Criticize yourself harshly and depend on external validation for self-worth.

This book is for teens and young adults who want to move beyond mediocrity and live with purpose. While reading this book, make it your own—highlight, underline, and write in the margins as things resonate with you.

Before diving into the eight habits of success, we'll explore "superfluous centers"—patterns that keep teens from living their best lives. The key to success is living by consistent principles, and that starts with clarifying your beliefs and values.

Being principle-centered means living by what you know is right, not following the crowd. When you choose values like honesty, kindness, and respect to guide you, life gets a lot clearer. Instead of worrying about what everyone else thinks or trying to fit in, you make decisions that actually feel good to you in the long run. This helps you feel more in control of your life because you're not reacting to drama or pressure—you're acting with intention. And when your choices match what you truly believe, you have far fewer regrets.

Living by your principles also builds self-confidence and self-esteem. Every time you assert your values, even when it's hard, you prove to yourself that you're strong and dependable. That kind of trust in yourself feels amazing. It underscores that you won't always need other people's approval to feel good. Teens who focus on what matters most instead of chasing popularity often end up with better friends, clearer goals, and less stress. Being principle-centered doesn't mean ignoring people. Instead, it means showing up as your real, best self. And that, my friend, is how you can build a successful life in which you're in control of your life.

SUPERFLUOUS CENTERS

*I*t can be challenging for teens to live consistently by their principles. Part of the reason for this is even adults often struggle to identify their own principles. We tend to react to events and emotions in the moment, moving from one situation to another without any clear focus. Another reason is our culture encourages us to be inconsistent, making it easier for them to sell us products and ideas.

In this chapter, you'll be invited to shift from a self-centered mindset to a principle-centered one. But first, it's important to examine what currently drives your actions. Are you self-centered? Other-centered? Or do you take time to reflect on how to act in different situations by reflecting on your beliefs and values?

If you're unsure, don't worry. Most of us don't realize how we make decisions until we pause and reflect. That's exactly what this chapter is meant to help you do.

What Is a Paradigm?

At this stage, I would like to introduce a new concept that will be helpful in understanding my habits of successful teens. This is the word "paradigm." A paradigm is essentially a lens through which we see ourselves, others, and the world. It shapes our perceptions, decisions, and behaviors. Often, our paradigms operate automatically, without our conscious awareness. To change self-defeating habits, however, we need to step back and examine these lenses.

Paradigms are like a pair of prescription glasses. If your glasses are worn upside down or are crooked on your nose, everything appears distorted. You may stumble or misjudge situations, and over time, you may even start believing this distorted version of reality. For example, if you think you're "stupid" or "incapable," you may start acting in ways that confirm that belief.

This is why wearing the right "lens" is so crucial. This right lens is a strong, principle-centered paradigm that allows you to navigate through life with clarity and purpose. Without it, unhealthy paradigms can limit your potential, while healthy ones can bring out your best qualities. Sometimes, you may need another person to act as a mirror to help you revise unhealthy perspectives.

Let me give you an example. In high school, I was a shy teen. I was convinced I couldn't perform in front of others. When auditions for a talent show came up and my English teacher encouraged me to participate, I refused. Then I was talking to my friend Natalie at lunch. She said she was going to audition, and she wanted me to do so with her. With her encouragement, I auditioned—and I performed well. We both got the role and enjoyed the whole experience. It helped both of us grow and become much more confident.

That experience changed my self-perception. I began to see myself not as a shy, incapable girl, but as someone capable of growth and achievement. This was an important time in my life as a shy and very uncertain teenager.

A good question to ask yourself is: Do your current mindsets and paradigms help or hinder you from becoming the best you can be? If they hold you back, this book will be your guide to make concrete changes in your life that are in line with who you truly are.

Many teens adopt paradigms that trap them into unhealthy patterns of behavior. These paradigms often reveal what is most important to us. Ask yourself a few key questions, such as: What gives you confidence? Do you idolize friends, material possessions, or technology? Do external influences dictate your actions?

Here are some common limiting paradigms:

1. Friend-Centered

If you base your self-worth on your friends' opinions or approval, you are friend-centered. Friends are important for support and enjoyment, but your identity should not depend on them. Be sure to take steps to develop your own beliefs and values rather than letting friendships define you.

2. Things-Centered

Do possessions define your happiness? If you rely on material items for self-worth, you may feel empty and unfulfilled. Your true confidence should be derived from within, not from what you own. Focus on developing internal strengths rather than chasing external validation through material possessions.

3. School-Centered

If your self-esteem depends on grades, academic recognition, or school status, you're school-centered. Education is important, but your identity should not be defined by it. Cultivate principles that give you a sense of purpose, independent of external achievements.

4. Technology-Centered

Do you rely heavily on phones, tablets, or other gadgets to feel accepted or entertained? If so, you are technology-centered. Overdependence on technology can harm both self-esteem and physical health. Instead, learn to prioritize real-world connections and develop confidence without constant digital validation.

5. Media-Centered

Many teens measure themselves against media standards—fashion, movies, or social trends. If your sense of worth comes from what the media promotes, you are media-centered. Remember, the media primarily aims to sell products, not guide principles. True fulfillment comes from internal growth, not fleeting trends.

6. Parent-Centered

Some teens derive all their self-worth from parental approval. While parents can be loving and guiding, our identity should not be controlled by them either. Developing your own beliefs and boundaries is essential for becoming an independently empowered individual.

I know firsthand how challenging this can be. My mother wanted me to live by her values, which made asserting my independence difficult. With support from mentors and counselors, I eventually set boundaries and embraced my own identity. This is a crucial step for any teen navigating expectations from parents, peers, and society.

7. Sport-Centered

Teens who base their self-esteem on athletic success are sport-centered. While sports can build skills and confidence, tying your identity to wins and losses creates instability. I learned this myself as a basketball player. When our team lost, my self-worth plummeted. True self-esteem comes from internal consistency, not external outcomes such as the score of a basketball game.

Building Your Own Identity

As we've seen, basing your identity on things outside of yourself, such as friends, possessions, media, parents, or sports, can leave you fragmented and insecure. The teen years are full of challenges to self-esteem and self-confidence, but you can navigate them by developing principles, values, and beliefs that are uniquely your own.

By cultivating inner confidence and living according to your chosen principles, you will gain control over your life. You will no longer need to rely on external validation. Instead, your identity will become stable, resilient, and aligned with who you truly are.

Conclusion: Choosing Principle-Centered Living

Therefore, stepping away from superfluous centers and toward a principle-centered life is one of the most powerful decisions you can make as a teen. The transition may feel uncomfortable at first because it means letting go of old habits, outdated mindsets, and the approval of others as your guiding focus. But your reward will be freedom from the constant pressure to measure up to shifting standards and the freedom to live with clarity and direction.

Thus, when you choose to anchor your life in principles rather than trends, relationships, or achievements, you choose stability. Principles don't change with fads or moods. They remain consistent even as your friends come and go, your grades fluctuate, or your phone loses its charge. They offer you a trustworthy framework for making decisions that align with your values rather than the loudest voices outside of you.

This chapter has invited you to examine the paradigms that currently shape your life and recognize which ones may be holding you back. You've seen how friend-centered, media-centered, and even parent-centered living can leave you feeling disconnected from your true self. Shifting to a principle-centered paradigm doesn't mean ignoring your friends, parents, or passions. It simply means allowing your core values to take the lead so your relationships and activities enhance your life instead of undermining it.

As you move forward, take the time to reflect on which principles matter most to you. Is it integrity, compassion, perseverance, faith, creativity, or kindness? Write them down, keep them visible, and revisit them often. When faced with tough choices, ask yourself, "Does this decision reflect my principles?" Over time, this practice will strengthen your confidence, shape your character, and help you grow into the person you are meant to be.

The journey toward principle-centered living is ongoing, but it begins with one choice: the choice to live from the inside out. Start today by noticing the "centers" that influence you most and taking a small step toward grounding your identity in principles that will guide you through the teenage years—and well beyond.

The eight habits discussed in this book can become your principles for living a resilient and successful life. They could become your foundation for success, helping you live in accordance with your beliefs and values and not by all the external voices around you.

HABIT I

Be Proactive Instead of Reactive

*B*eing principle-centered means acting from your inner values rather than reacting impulsively to circumstances. Proactive behavior is guided by beliefs and thoughtful decisions, whereas reactive behavior is driven by emotion and external events. Developing the habit of being proactive takes effort, but the payoff is significant.

Reactive individuals respond to life's pressures impulsively, like a shaken-up pop can that explodes under stress. They may yell, curse, or lash out without considering their values. This approach often stems from unresolved anger, a feeling of victimhood, or a lack of clarity about our personal beliefs. Reactive people are typically people pleasers, letting others' actions dictate their emotions.

In contrast, proactive people act according to their principles and values. They pause before reacting, recognize what they can control, and focus on solutions rather than problems. They respond calmly, even under pressure, maintaining composure like water— unshaken even when disturbed.

How you respond to setbacks, whether it's a bad grade, a difficult conversation, or a minor accident, reflects your level of emotional intelligence. Proactive responses involve thoughtfulness, reflection, and solution-seeking, whereas reactive responses often involve immediate anger or frustration.

Ask yourself: Are you reactive or proactive in challenging situations? If you don't know the answer to the question, try to observe your behavior over a few weeks. Identify triggers and patterns. Awareness is the first step toward change.

Reactive people are often situation-driven, letting circumstances dictate their mood and behavior.

This creates instability and prevents effective coping. Proactive people, on the other hand, identify opportunities, anticipate challenges, and act constructively, even in difficult circumstances.

For example, if another driver cuts you off, a reactive response might involve cursing or honking, while a proactive response involves staying calm and moving on, conserving energy for more important matters.

Living proactively fosters accomplishment, control, and emotional balance. It allows you to cope effectively with setbacks and interact positively with others. To cultivate proactive behavior, consider these strategies:

1. **Take responsibility:** Recognize that only you can control your actions and behavior.

2. **Focus on solutions:** Instead of panicking when setbacks occur, analyze the situation and respond constructively.

3. **Avoid gossip:** Step back from hurtful situations, reflect objectively, and seek solutions rather than dwelling on negativity.

4. **Find lessons in challenges:** Difficult situations can reveal insights about yourself and guide future decisions.

5. **Rise above abuse:** Step back, examine the situation calmly, learn from it, and move forward.

6. **Pause when overwhelmed:** Give yourself space to regain control and perspective.

7. **Replace negative self-talk:** Write down your negative thoughts and replace them with positive ones.

8. **Forgive mistakes:** Accept your errors, learn from them, and move forward without self-criticism.

The teen years can be emotionally turbulent, but practicing proactive, principle-centered responses creates stability. By mastering this habit, you can maintain control over your reactions, strengthen emotional intelligence, and navigate life with composure and clarity.

Adolescence can feel like a roller-coaster, with your emotions feeling out of whack, friends acting unpredictably, and life throwing curve balls left and right. That's why developing the habit of being proactive instead of reactive is such a game changer. When you act based on your values instead of letting every situation dictate your mood, you can take control of your life instead of letting life control you.

Being proactive means pausing before you react, thinking things through, and choosing responses that match who you want to become. It's about realizing that while you can't always control what happens to you, you *can* always control how you respond. Every time you choose calm over anger, solutions over complaints, or reflection over panic, you're building emotional strength and stability.

Reactive behavior might feel like the easier path in the moment, such as yelling, lashing out, or blaming others. However, it drains your energy and leaves you stuck in a cycle of frustration. Proactivity, on the other hand, sets you up to handle anything life throws at you.

Being proactive can also help you handle challenges, strengthen your relationships, and boost your confidence. It turns setbacks into lessons, mistakes into growth, and stress into opportunity. Whether it's a fight with a friend, a disappointing grade, or a curveball in life, taking a proactive approach lets you stay calm, think clearly, and move forward without getting derailed.

At the end of the day, being proactive is about owning your actions and your life. It's about steering your journey instead of being tossed around by every little wave. The teen years may be messy, but mastering this habit gives you control, confidence, and clarity. When you commit to acting from your values, you don't only survive, but you thrive. Proactivity isn't just a habit for today; it's the foundation for the adult you're becoming.

HABIT 2
Constantly Renew and Evolve

*D*uring your teen years, it's easy to stay stuck in the same routines and avoid growth. Remaining stagnant means repeating the same behaviors—even when they don't work—and expecting different results. Growth occurs most notably when you actively seek to renew yourself, develop new habits, and try things differently. Your teen years are a perfect time to build healthy habits that can last a lifetime.

This second habit is about evolving into a motivated, mature, and self-empowered adult with strong leadership qualities. By constantly renewing yourself, you can live a fulfilling life, make emotionally intelligent decisions, and cope with challenges calmly.

Here are seven ways to help you grow and evolve:

1. Take Stock Often

Reflect regularly on where you are and where you want to go. Taking stock helps you assess progress and make adjustments. Without it, you may feel lost or uncertain about your next steps. Treat it as a self-assessment tool to guide your growth.

2. Change One Small Irrational Behavior at a Time

Trying to change too much all at once can be overwhelming. Start with one habit that isn't serving you, like bingeing on snacks when frustrated, and then commit to changing it over a few weeks. Once successful, move to the next habit. Use your journal to track your progress, set goals, and reflect on challenges.

3. Rise Above Mediocrity

It's easy to blend in, but striving for excellence sets you apart. Youth gives you energy and opportunity. Don't waste it by settling for "being ordinary." Instead, focus on being your best in school, sports, hobbies, and relationships. Even small acts of excellence can have a lasting impact.

4. Learn to Control Your Attitudes

Your attitudes shape your life. Negative attitudes make life harder, while positive, resilient ones can help you thrive. Don't let situations or people dictate your feelings. Practice self-awareness and choose responses that reflect your values and goals, instead of peer pressure or media influence.

5. Become an Agent of Change

You don't have to emulate your family's unhealthy habits or accept dysfunction as normal. Identify negative patterns, like anger, poor nutrition, or laziness, and make sure that you try to do things differently. Seek guidance or mentoring when needed. Making intentional changes builds resilience and self-confidence.

6. Press the Pause Button

When someone provokes or frustrates you, step back instead of reacting. Pause to observe your thoughts, listen to your conscience, imagine solutions, and act with willpower. This practice strengthens emotional control and helps you respond wisely, even under pressure.

7. Find a Place of Refuge

Everyone needs a personal space to recharge. Whether it's a corner in your room, a park bench, or a quiet study area, having a place to reflect, relax, and reconnect with yourself is crucial. Learning to enjoy your own company helps you build self-acceptance and independence.

This habit is all about taking charge of your own growth. Your teen years are the perfect time to try new things, break old habits, and figure out who you really want to become. Growth doesn't happen automatically; we must make it happen. It starts with small steps, such as noticing what's working in your life, changing one behavior at a time, and refusing to settle for "just okay." Every choice you make will shape your path. So why not choose the ones that push you forward?

Being your best isn't about being perfect; it's about aiming higher than you did yesterday. It's about learning to manage your attitudes, respond instead of react, and rise above negativity, whether it comes from friends, social media, or even yourself. When you become an agent of change, you're saying "I will not be defined by old patterns of behavior or what's expected of me. I'll create my own rules."

And don't forget to hit pause as often as you need. Stepping back when your emotions are raw or going into your quiet space to think and recharge isn't weakness—it's necessary. It helps you make better decisions, stay calm under pressure, and build confidence in your own judgment. These habits might seem small, but over time, they add up and lead to real, lasting growth.

Therefore, constant renewal isn't a one-time thing. It's a mindset—a way of living. It's about curiosity, courage, and the willingness to keep moving, even when change is uncomfortable. By choosing to evolve, you're not just surviving your teen years. You're shaping the kind of person you want to become for life. Every day is a chance to reflect, learn, and take action. And with each step forward, you're building a stronger, wiser, and more confident you.

So don't wait for change to find you. Go out and make it happen. Keep growing, evolving, and becoming the person only you can be.

HABIT 3
Be a Go-Getter

Our teen years are usually riddled with a lot of frustration and anxiety. Life often feels unfair, and it's easy to develop a whining or complaining attitude. I remember my own teenage struggles vividly. But here's the truth: Complaining keeps us stuck in negativity. It wastes energy and changes nothing. To thrive, we must shift our mindset from whining to winning.

Being a go-getter means channeling your energy into action rather than complaining. It starts with accepting your current situation and doing your best to make it better. A go-getter focuses on solutions, not problems. Change is a part of life, and embracing it is essential for growth. Over time, this proactive attitude will transform you into someone who doesn't simply wait for things to happen—but one who makes them happen.

A go-getter goes above and beyond the minimum. She exceeds expectations and puts forth her best effort in everything she does. Being called a go-getter reflects your ambition, dedication, and perseverance.

There are five key traits of go-getters: (1) being receptive, (2) going beyond the minimum, (3) being high achievers, (4) managing our time effectively, and (5) committing fully. Let's explore these traits.

1. Being receptive means being open to new ideas, feedback, and new knowledge. A receptive person:

- **Receives knowledge**: Actively takes in information and applies it constructively.

- **Seeks new ideas**: Is always curious, reading, and learning.

- **Welcomes suggestions**: Is open-minded and willing to try new ways of acting and doing things.

- **Becomes a lifelong learner**: Is continuously seeking to improve, evolve, and stay informed.

- **Is inquisitive**: Asks questions, looks for the truth, and refuses to settle for ignorance.

- **Listens actively**: Pays full attention, empathizes, and responds thoughtfully.

Therefore, receptive people thrive. Non-receptive people, on the other hand, remain stagnant, doing the same things repeatedly, closing themselves off from growth.

2. It's easy to do just enough to get by. But excellence comes from doing more than expected. Going beyond the minimum:

- **Boosts our self-confidence**: Doing something well gives you pride and recognition.

- **Encourages continuous improvement**: You always look for ways to do something better.

- **Rejects second best**: Strives for being the personal best instead of settling for mediocrity.

- **Builds self-esteem**: Take pride in work that is well done. This strengthens character and can inspire others to also excel.

3. High achievers are goal-oriented, disciplined, and internally driven. They:

- Set clear goals and pursue them diligently.

- Focus on self-improvement rather than comparing themselves to others (which is a waste of time and energy).

- Work hard consistently, understanding that success requires effort over time.

- Organizes their time effectively to achieve maximum results.

I had a friend in my teens who exemplified this perfectly. Her dedication inspired me to follow her example, inspiring me to excel academically and win scholarships. These habits shaped my confidence and carried me through university and beyond.

4. Time management is crucial. Go-getters prioritize their goals, plan their actions, and follow through consistently. The skills we develop as a teen will carry us into our adult life. May they be healthy ones.

5. Being a go-getter isn't here only in one moment and then gone. It requires consistent energy, discipline, and a positive mindset. Try to surround yourself with positive people, focus on excellence, and embrace challenges.

By adopting these habits, you can transform your life from a passive observer of life into an empowered doer. Shifting from negativity to positivism, exceeding expectations, and striving for achievement will set you apart. Being a go-getter isn't only about success—it's about becoming the best version of yourself.

Teen life can feel frustrating, unfair, and out of your control. Complaining might seem like a release at the time, but it changes nothing. Being a go-getter is about changing that narrative and channeling your energy into action, solutions, and growth. It's about taking charge of your life instead of waiting for things to happen.

A go-getter starts by being receptive and being open to learning, listening, and trying new ideas. Growth comes to those who stay curious, embrace feedback, and refuse to settle for ignorance. Next, they go beyond the minimum. Doing just enough won't set us apart. However, pushing ourselves builds confidence, pride, and momentum. High achievers set clear goals, work hard consistently, and focus on improving themselves, not comparing to others. Managing our time is crucially important. We must prioritize, plan, and follow through. And above all, we must commit fully. Being a go-getter is a habit we can develop; however, it must become a way of life.

What makes this habit powerful is its ripple effect. Every small choice we make, such as seeking feedback, exceeding expectations, and staying disciplined, shapes who we will become. The skills we build now will follow us into school, work, and adult life. They turn frustration into motivation, obstacles into opportunities, and ordinary effort into extraordinary results.

Being a go-getter isn't only about winning trophies, getting high grades, or earning recognition. It's about becoming the person you're capable of being, resilient, ambitious, and unstoppable. By choosing action over complaints, solutions over excuses, and growth over comfort, you step into your own power. The teen years are the perfect time to start. The earlier you start living this way, the more resilient you'll feel.

Go-getters don't wait for life to give them what they want. Instead, they take steps to make it happen. Start now, take charge, and watch yourself become the best version of you.

HABIT 4
Determine Your Beliefs and Values

*F*iguring out your beliefs and values can feel challenging at first. It's often easier to follow the crowd by doing what your friends do and acting in accordance with popular opinions. But if you only follow others all the time, you'll risk losing sight of who you truly are. Knowing your beliefs and values is essential to living authentically. Without that, you won't understand what drives you, and your life can feel ungrounded and inauthentic.

So what do you truly believe in? What matters most to you? If you're unsure, try writing your thoughts down in a journal. Start by identifying your core values—they don't have to be religious or spiritual, but they can be. Values are simply the principles that guide your actions and the qualities you admire in yourself and others.

For example, I value kindness, generosity, honesty, curiosity, and love. These values shape my beliefs. So, for example, if I value kindness, I believe in treating others with compassion. If I value learning, I believe in lifelong education. Take some time to reflect on what matters to you and write it down. Don't worry if it doesn't come to you immediately. It can take some time to engage in this type of reflection.

Here are some ways to discover your beliefs and values.

1. Turn Inward Regularly

It's easy to get distracted by technology and the busyness of life. But to truly know yourself, you need quiet time to listen to your intuition or inner voice. It will signal your comfort, discomfort, and reactions to people or situations. Your intuition knows you better than anyone else, and learning to become aware of it is the key to understanding your values.

2. Identify Your Likes and Dislikes

Your teenage years are filled with trial and error. You might enjoy something one week and suddenly dislike it. Still, observing your patterns of behavior can reveal your true likes. Ask yourself, which activities consistently make me happy? What situations drain or upset me? Your long-term likes and dislikes often point directly to your core values.

3. Reflect On Your Long-Term Patterns of Behavior

Your values will become obvious over time. For example, volunteering at a homeless shelter might initially feel exciting. But if you give up at the first challenge you experience, it wasn't yet a deeply held value but just a temporary interest. Values are consistent, guiding choices even when situations are tough.

4. Observe Your Actions

Pay attention to how you act in everyday life. Your behaviors often reflect your beliefs and values more accurately than words alone. If you're upset when someone is treated unfairly, it shows you value justice. If you like helping others, generosity may be central to your beliefs.

5. Connect Your Beliefs and Actions

Your beliefs can often be derived from your actions. Write down your habitual behaviors, likes, and dislikes, then reflect on them. Over time, patterns will emerge, revealing your core principles. In fact, this is a sign of a successful life.

Although the teen years can be confusing, they can also be a time of immense self-discovery and joy. By understanding your beliefs and values, you can make choices that align with who you really are, creating a more empowered, meaningful, and stable life. Getting to know yourself is the first step.

Ultimately, determining your beliefs and values isn't simply an exercise—it's the foundation for a life that feels true to you. When you know what matters most, every decision becomes easier, every challenge more navigable, and every success more fulfilling. Teens who take the time to define their principles aren't just drifting along through life. They're steering their own lives with intention. You begin to notice a shift: Peer pressure loses its power, fleeting trends become less distracting, and you start standing up for what matters, even when it's difficult.

Further, this habit isn't about perfection or having all the answers immediately. Your beliefs and values may evolve as you grow, and that's natural. The important thing to remember is to be conscious and deliberate, choosing to explore, question, and understand yourself rather than letting life's relentless noise of your life dictate your path. The more you take the time to reflect, observe, and align your actions with your principles, the more confident you'll become in the choices you make in your life. You'll start living with purpose instead of reacting to what others expect.

Living by your values also transforms how you interact with the world. Your relationships will deepen because people will sense your authenticity. Opportunities become clearer because you can distinguish what aligns with your principles and what doesn't. You'll feel grounded. This feeling of inner stability will guide you through the chaos of teenage life and beyond.

So take the time to look inward, notice patterns in your behavior, and identify what truly matters. Write these down, talk about them, and test them in real-life situations. The effort you put into knowing yourself now will pay off. You'll become more resilient, gain clarity, and build a life on your own terms. Determining your beliefs and values isn't just a habit—it's a lifelong compass that will help you navigate every twist and turn ahead with courage, clarity, and confidence.

HABIT 5

Develop Autonomy Through Boundaries

O nce you become aware of your beliefs and values, the next step is putting them into practice. Remember, empowerment starts from within, not from the approval of others. By acting autonomously, you will control your actions and decisions because they will be based on your principles rather than the fleeting desires of your peers. Autonomy doesn't mean doing whatever you want in any given moment. However, it does mean consistently acting in alignment with your values and beliefs.

Acting autonomously during your teen years takes a lot of courage. It often means resisting peer pressure, standing firm even when others disapprove, and accepting that not everyone will like you. Autonomy requires relying on your long-term beliefs and values as a guide, which is where your boundaries come in. Boundaries help protect your beliefs, energy, and sense of self, allowing you to act in alignment with who you truly are.

A boundary is like a protective shield that keeps you intact. Without boundaries, others can undermine your beliefs, values, and sense of self. There are several types of boundaries you can develop to strengthen your autonomy: emotional, feeling, value, belief, and thought boundaries.

Emotional Boundaries

Emotional boundaries help protect your heart from being hurt repeatedly. If you came from an abusive home environment or have been emotionally manipulated, it's vital to maintain distance from a person until you feel safe. Forgive others, but protect yourself from repeated harm. Only you can care for your emotional well-being.

Feeling Boundaries

Feeling boundaries help you express emotions safely. Not everyone will respond positively to your feelings, so carefully choose who you share them with. Your feelings are signals about your relationships. They will tell you when something is going well and if something needs your attention. Honor your feelings and use them to guide your choices.

Value Boundaries

Value boundaries ensure that you act according to what matters most to you. Teens often seek approval from peers, but living according to others' expectations undermines your autonomy. Take responsibility for your choices, assert your values, and don't let others override them. By doing so, you'll gain self-control and empowerment.

Belief Boundaries

Beliefs shape how you see yourself, others, and the world. People without strong belief boundaries often blame others for their discomfort instead of owning their attitudes. Know your beliefs, examine them critically, and stand by them in everyday situations. Your convictions define your autonomy.

Thought Boundaries

Thought boundaries protect your mind from being dominated by the ideas of others. To establish your boundaries:

1. **Own your thoughts:** Question assumptions and opinions you inherit from others. Think for yourself.

2. **Grow in knowledge:** Understand your values and act accordingly.

3. **Clarify distortions:** Check your perceptions of people and situations. Communicate your thoughts clearly—don't expect others to read your mind.

Establishing and maintaining boundaries is challenging, but the result is a life lived autonomously. By protecting your heart, feelings, values, beliefs, and thoughts, you empower yourself to act with confidence, courage, and integrity. Autonomous teens grow into autonomous adults who honor their beliefs and values.

The Power of Boundaries and Autonomy

Developing autonomy through boundaries is not just a skill—it's a way of life. Boundaries are the framework that supports your independence, self-respect, and confidence. They allow you to navigate relationships and challenges without losing sight of who you are. The teen years are full of uncertainty, peer pressure, and emotional turbulence, which makes boundaries even more essential. When you establish and maintain strong boundaries, you create a safe space for your values, beliefs, feelings, and thoughts to thrive.

Autonomy is about more than resisting pressure from others. It is about understanding yourself deeply and choosing to act in alignment with that understanding. It requires courage, practice, and sometimes patience with yourself when you falter. There will be times when asserting your boundaries feels uncomfortable or when others push against them. That is normal. Growth is rarely smooth. What matters most is that you continue to act in accordance with your principles, even when it's hard. Each time you assert a boundary, you strengthen your sense of self and reinforce the foundation for living your life on your own terms.

It's also important to remember that boundaries are not barriers meant to isolate you. Instead, they are tools for healthy relationships. By setting clear limits, you protect yourself from harm while allowing genuine connections with people who respect your values and honor your feelings. Over time, you will find that autonomy and boundaries will actually work together to improve your relationships, because you'll interact from a place of honesty and integrity rather than fear or compliance.

Acting autonomously by honoring your boundaries is a lifelong practice. As you grow, your values and beliefs may evolve, and your boundaries will need to adapt. What remains constant is the principle of acting intentionally and protecting your inner self. The more you act autonomously, the more resilient, confident, and empowered you will become. You'll learn that fitting in is never as rewarding as standing firm in who you truly are.

Ultimately, the power of autonomy lies in the freedom it gives you. When you honor your boundaries, you live a life guided by your own values, not by the expectations or whims of others. You gain the ability to make decisions that reflect your authentic self, and you discover a sense of empowerment that can't be taken away. By protecting your heart, your feelings, values, beliefs, and thoughts, you lay the groundwork for living with integrity, purpose, and self-respect.

Autonomous teens become autonomous adults. By committing to these principles now, you are investing in a future where your choices, actions, and relationships are rooted in truth and authenticity. Boundaries are not restrictions. Instead, they are your passport to freedom, empowerment, and a life fully lived. Start small, practice consistently, and watch as your autonomy grows stronger with each decision you make. In the end, the most valuable gift you can give yourself is the ability to live confidently, courageously, and autonomously.

HABIT 6
Be Your Best

To be your best means striving for excellence in everything you do. "Your best" will look different depending on your circumstances. Your goal is to always be improving. This is the essence of personal growth and resilience. Being your best requires raising the bar a little at a time, constantly recreating yourself, and rethinking who you are as you evolve. This prevents stagnation and mediocrity, keeping you motivated and engaged in life.

Here are eight tips to help you be your best and stretch beyond your comfort zone.

1. Expect to Be Your Best

It's easy to drift through life on autopilot, especially when your friends are doing the same. Mediocrity becomes comfortable, but it isn't fulfilling. Surrounding yourself with positive and inspiring people can help you aim higher.

Being proactive rather than passive in your life is the most important habit you can foster in order to live a successful life. Passive individuals react to life, blaming circumstances or others when things don't go their way. A proactive teen, however, takes charge, anticipating challenges, making things happen, and striving for excellence. This proactive mindset takes courage and practice to develop, but it sets the stage for living your best life.

2. Change a Stagnant Mindset

Growth begins with a shift in perspective. Ask yourself: Are my current beliefs and habits helping me grow, or are they keeping me stuck? Do I wait for things to happen rather than take control of what I can and release what I cannot? With discipline and practice, you can transform your mindset from passive to proactive, which is essential for becoming your best.

3. Keep Stretching Yourself

Falling into routine is normal, but habitual inertia leads to mediocrity. To rise above, challenge yourself continuously. Try new activities, learn new skills, read widely, volunteer, and step outside of your comfort zone. By experimenting and pushing your limits, you may discover hidden talents and passions.

4. Don't Compete with Others

Your journey is unique. Comparing yourself to others only distracts you from your own potential. Also, it wastes time and energy. Focus on your strengths, explore what you enjoy, and celebrate your growth. When you honor your gifts, you'll feel empowered without needing to measure yourself against anyone else.

5. Be Progressive

Being progressive means striving to be more than ordinary. It requires curiosity, open-mindedness, and self-reliance. Stand by your beliefs, make bold choices, and take initiative. Progressive thinkers are also broad-minded, willing to challenge conformity when necessary, and they consistently aim to improve themselves.

6. Break the Habit of Repetition

Doing the same thing repeatedly is stagnating. To grow, you must experiment with new approaches and activities. Try something different for a few weeks, evaluate the results, and keep refining. Growth requires continuous change, effort, and the willingness to leave comfort behind.

7. Take Pride in Your Efforts

Few feelings compare to the satisfaction of knowing you gave something your all. Pride strengthens self-esteem, motivates continual improvement, and builds resilience. Take the time to celebrate your achievements, large and small, and make striving for excellence a habit. Over time, this attitude will make you stronger, more confident, and empowered to handle challenges.

8. Put Positive Energy into Your Life

Negativity will drain your energy and cloud your focus. Cultivating positive thoughts fosters happiness, gratitude, and motivation. By focusing on the good and nurturing optimism, you increase your ability to excel. Positive energy is contagious. Your attitude will inspire those around you to be their best as well.

Being your best is not always easy. However, it's one of the most rewarding things you can do for yourself. Surround yourself with ambitious peers, stretch yourself beyond comfort, and take pride in every effort. Each step forward, no matter how small, will build momentum and confidence. The teen years can be challenging, but with consistent effort and the right mindset, you can rise above mediocrity and experience the satisfaction of being your best self.

Being your best is more than just achieving goals or earning praise—it's about committing to a mindset of growth, resilience, and self-respect. When you consistently strive to improve, even in small ways, you begin to build a foundation of confidence and self-worth that will carry you through challenges now and in the future. Every effort you make to be proactive, stretch yourself, or approach life with positivism is an investment in the person you are becoming.

Remember, being your best doesn't mean being perfect. Mistakes, setbacks, and failures are all part of your journey. What matters is your willingness to learn from them, adjust, and keep moving forward. Each time you rise above mediocrity, you create momentum that propels you toward even greater accomplishments.

Surround yourself with people who encourage and inspire you. Seek experiences that challenge you and expand your perspective. As often as you can, celebrate your victories, no matter how small, and take pride in the progress you make each day. Over time, these habits combined can shape you into someone who not only reaches personal goals but inspires others to do the same.

Ultimately, being your best is a lifelong commitment—to yourself, your values, and your dreams. It's about living intentionally, embracing challenges, and constantly evolving into a stronger, more capable, and more confident version of yourself. By applying this habit daily, you can transform your life one step, one choice, and one effort at a time.

Habit 7

Be Authentic

Being authentic requires that we live in alignment with our deepest beliefs and desires. It requires the courage to speak our truth with compassion and conviction, to say yes when we mean yes, and no when we mean no. Authenticity also requires that we know what makes our eyes sparkle and deliberately seek experiences that nourish that joy. Over time, this deep self-awareness builds a life of meaning, purpose, and genuine happiness.

Authenticity also grows from self-love. It is treating ourselves with kindness, recognizing our worth, and giving ourselves grace when we make mistakes. It involves releasing the need for external approval and resisting people-pleasing for the sake of acceptance. Self-love involves protecting our energy, honoring our intuition, and nurturing our spirit. It is an inner joy, an unshakable appreciation for who we are, and it deepens as we connect with our true selves.

Living authentically means making choices guided by intuition, understanding that we are the captains of our own ship, and prioritizing our values over the expectations of others. While it can take practice, the rewards we gain are immeasurable. We can feel more confident and fulfilled during our teen years, and that is very important given the tremulousness of these early years of our lives.

Here are some ways to become more authentic.

1. Be Courageous

Being ourselves requires bravery. Courage means showing the world who we truly are, even if it risks rejection. True friends accept us for who we are, not for who they want us to be. When we stop seeking universal approval, we invite authentic connections.

2. Listen to Your Heart

Turn inward often to hear your intuition. In a world full of distractions, this may take practice. Pay attention to moments when you feel uneasy or unsure. This often signals from your intuition that something is wrong.

3. Trust Your Inner Voice

Listening is only the first step; trust is essential. Even when peers or media tell us otherwise, our inner voice carries wisdom unique to us. Honoring it builds confidence in our decisions.

4. Develop a Passionate Life

Go beyond the minimum in all your pursuits. Live with gratitude, kindness, and enthusiasm. Seek experiences that excite and inspire you to be your best. Passion transforms ordinary living into a life of fulfillment.

5. Make Values-Based Choices

Align your decisions with your beliefs, and don't cave in to peer pressure. Knowing your principles gives clarity in uncertain times and strengthens your authenticity.

6. Discover What Brings True Joy

Explore your interests and pleasures step-by-step. Notice what makes you smile, what inspires you, and what brings you meaning. Prioritize the activities that make you feel good.

7. Be the Captain of Your Ship

Take control of your life. Assert your values, speak up for yourself, and resist letting others steer your path. By shifting your choices so they are in line with your beliefs and values, you will strengthen your identity and self-esteem.

Authenticity is a journey, not a destination. By being courageous, listening to and trusting our hearts, pursuing passion, making values-aligned choices, discovering joy, and steering our own ship, we cultivate a life that reflects our truest selves. The road may be challenging, but the reward—a confident, joyful, and meaningful life—is worth every effort.

Living an authentic life is not always easy. It takes courage, self-awareness, and a willingness to face discomfort. Society, peers, and even family can sometimes pressure us to conform. But every time we choose to honor our beliefs and values, we become more resilient and confident. Authenticity is not a single act; it is a lifestyle, a series of decisions that align with our values, beliefs, and desires. It begins with small choices and grows into a powerful way of living that permeates every aspect of our lives.

One of the most important lessons of being authentic is learning to navigate the tension between who we are and who others expect us to be. This can be especially challenging during the teenage years, when fitting in often feels more important than being true to ourselves. Yet, the more we practice being authentic now, the more naturally it will come to us in adulthood. Each time we resist external pressure, and each time we honor our beliefs and values, we're training ourselves to live with integrity, self-respect, and confidence in our adult years.

Living authentically also requires that we regularly pause and ask ourselves some difficult questions, such as "Am I acting in alignment with my values?" or "Does this choice honor who I truly am?" Such questions build integrity and autonomy. Living authentically is what helps us create a successful life that will be with us right into our adult years. Reflection can also help us understand our motivations, desires, and boundaries, empowering us to make conscious decisions rather than reacting impulsively to external demands. Over time, this self-awareness becomes a compass, guiding us through both small everyday choices and major life decisions.

Another vital aspect of authenticity is learning to embrace our imperfections. We may fear that being true to ourselves will expose flaws, weaknesses, or unpopular opinions. But authenticity is not about perfection. Instead, it's about honesty and courage. It means acknowledging our mistakes, forgiving ourselves, and growing from each experience. It also means recognizing that our uniqueness is a strength. No one else has our combination of experiences, perspectives, and talents. By embracing who we are fully, we create space to contribute our gifts to the world in ways that no one else can.

Authenticity strengthens relationships as well. When we are true to ourselves, we attract people who value us for who we are rather than who we pretend to be. This fosters deeper, more meaningful connections. It also teaches others around us the value of authenticity, creating a ripple effect of courage, honesty, and integrity. True friends respect our boundaries, celebrate our achievements, and support our growth.

of inner harmony and integrity, which is the foundation of healthy self-esteem.

Authenticity requires honesty—both with yourself and the world around you. It means acknowledging what matters most to you and being willing to express it, even when it feels uncomfortable. Each time you choose to speak your truth or act in alignment with your values, you send yourself a powerful message: *I matter. My voice counts.* This self-validation slowly replaces the need for constant external validation.

Over time, living authentically strengthens your self-respect and self-trust. You no longer feel the pressure to perform or wear a mask, and that freedom allows your confidence to grow naturally. You begin to see yourself not as someone who must prove their worth, but as someone who is already enough—just as you are.

If you're looking to boost your self-esteem, start by asking yourself where you might be holding back your true thoughts, feelings, or desires. Then take one small step toward living more in line with your authentic self. Even tiny acts of truth-telling can lead to a deep sense of pride and self-worth.

I turn to the importance of living authentically and building self-esteem in the final habit.

HABIT 8

Live Authentically and Build Self-Esteem

*I*t cannot be highlighted enough that being a teen is challenging. The pressures of school, peers, social media, and family can make it feel like we're constantly trying to fit into someone else's expectations. Yet the most empowering choice we can make is to turn inward and develop a sense of self that is independent, strong, and authentic. Living by this new paradigm—one that prioritizes our own beliefs, values, and desires over external validation—is key to becoming confident, resilient, and emotionally intelligent.

When our identity is shaped by parents, peers, sports, or school activities rather than by our own beliefs, we risk losing touch with our true selves. More than that, our self-worth becomes dependent on others' opinions. This dependence can erode confidence, create low self-esteem, and make it difficult to recognize who we truly are. How we feel about ourselves directly impacts our actions. If we feel uncertain, awkward, or unworthy, our responses to challenges will reflect that. By becoming inward-guided rather than outward-guided, we begin to act from a place of confidence and clarity rather than reaction and anxiety.

The good news is our self-esteem can be nurtured one action and decision at a time. Every choice either honors or undermines our sense of self. Acting in alignment with our values strengthens self-esteem, while acting against them weakens it. Ultimately, building self-trust is central. Do we have the courage to act on our principles even when challenged? How do we respond to peer pressure, criticism, or conflict? How we navigate these situations reveals the strength and resilience of our inner selves.

Here are some signs of low self-esteem and healthy self-esteem.

Low self-esteem often arises when we:

- Constantly give in to peer pressure
- Are overconcerned about what others think
- Act arrogantly to hide our insecurities
- Compare ourselves to others
- Use drugs and alcohol to cope with feelings

Healthy self-esteem, on the other hand, is reflected when we:

- Stand up for ourselves and our beliefs
- Trust our inner judgment
- Pursue our personal goals without needing approval
- Celebrate others' successes without jealousy
- Maintain a positive outlook and enjoy our own company

Building Self-Esteem from the Inside Out

Developing self-esteem from the inside out is about centering ourselves on our own values and beliefs rather than external approval. Social popularity or fitting in may feel important, but true self-esteem comes from consistent inward-guided practice.

Here are some steps to cultivate inner strength.

1. Clarify Your Views

Reflect on your position regarding important issues, such as your friendships, substance use, social behavior, and the types of people you feel comfortable surrounding yourself with. Awareness of your preferences helps you make choices that support your authentic self.

2. Identify Your Beliefs and Values

Journaling or thoughtful reflection can uncover what matters most to you. Acting in alignment with your values strengthens self-trust and helps you respond to life's challenges with confidence.

3. Keep Promises to Yourself

Follow through on commitments, even small ones. This builds reliability and reinforces belief in your own abilities. Start with manageable goals and gradually take on larger challenges.

4. Practice Honesty

Be truthful with yourself and others. Authenticity fosters wholeness, strengthens relationships, and cultivates respect for your own identity.

5. Renew Yourself Regularly

Create personal space to recharge. Whether it's in a room, on a walk in nature, or in a quiet corner, taking time for reflection and renewal allows you to reconnect with your thoughts, feelings, and passions.

6. Enjoy Your Own Company

Learning to be comfortable alone strengthens self-reliance and introspection. It can also provide clarity, build resilience, and foster self-discovery.

7. Develop Personal Hobbies and Interests

Pursuing activities you genuinely enjoy helps you discover your passions and uniqueness. Avoid following the crowd blindly; instead, explore experiences that truly resonate with you.

Living By a New Paradigm

This new paradigm I've been discussing at length throughout this book is about shifting our perspective from outward-directness to inward-guided living. Instead of relying on external validation, you should take steps to center your life on your own values, beliefs, and desires. This approach builds self-knowledge, resilience, and emotional intelligence. It also empowers you to navigate social pressures, technological distractions, and peer influences with confidence.

The teen years are not just a social period. They can also be a time for you to joyously discover who you truly are. By practicing inward-guided living now, you lay the foundation for a fulfilling adult life. This involves courage, self-reflection, and daily choices that honor your authentic self. Carving out time to reflect, renew, and enjoy your own company strengthens your inner life, making you more empowered and resilient.

Living authentically and building self-esteem is not a one-time achievement; it is a lifelong practice. It begins with small, intentional actions taken consistently over time—actions that honor your values, beliefs, and inner voice. Each choice to act from your beliefs and values will strengthen your confidence, build self-trust, and deepen your understanding of who you truly are. The teen years are the perfect time to start this practice because habits formed now will set the tone for your adult life.

Authenticity requires courage. It asks us to stand firm in our beliefs, speak our truth, and act in alignment with our values, even when it feels uncomfortable. It asks us to resist peer pressure, external expectations, and social comparisons. Choosing this path may mean being misunderstood or even rejected by some, but the rewards far outweigh the discomfort. When you live authentically, you attract relationships, opportunities, and experiences that honor the real you, not a version shaped by others. True friends and mentors celebrate your strengths, encourage your growth, and support your unique journey.

Your self-esteem is intrinsically connected to your authenticity. When you honor your values and act with integrity, your self-respect will strengthen and you'll become more resilient. This inner confidence allows you to face life's challenges with resilience, recover from setbacks without losing your sense of worth, and approach each new situation with clarity

Finally, living authentically brings lasting joy and fulfillment. When our choices align with our values, we no longer waste energy trying to meet others' expectations. Life becomes more vibrant, purposeful, and joyful. The sparkle in our eyes—the excitement, curiosity, and passion that arise from living in alignment with our heart—is the most reliable indicator that we are on the right path.

In short, becoming authentic is a lifelong practice. It requires courage, self-love, reflection, and resilience. But the rewards you'll receive are immeasurable. You will become confident, enjoy meaningful relationships, gain clarity and purpose in your life, and experience a profound sense of joy. By embracing authenticity during our teenage years, we lay the groundwork for a life that is not only successful but deeply fulfilling—a life that truly belongs to us.

Living authentically builds self-esteem. Self-esteem doesn't come from external approval, success, or fitting into someone else's expectations—it comes from living in alignment with who you truly are. When you live authentically, you make choices based on your values, passions, and needs rather than trying to meet the standards of others. This creates a sense and courage. Self-esteem developed from the inside out is unshakable. It's not dependent on the approval, accolades, or external validation from others. Instead, it is a reflection of the deep knowing that you are capable, worthy, and deserving of respect and joy.

Developing self-esteem and authenticity also means embracing self-knowledge. Taking time to reflect, enjoying your own company, exploring hobbies, and identifying what brings you true joy are essential. Solitude is not loneliness. Instead, it's an opportunity to connect with your inner self, listen to your heart, and discover your passions. Each moment spent in honest self-reflection strengthens your ability to make rational decisions that are in alignment with your beliefs and values. This will help you live with integrity.

Finally, living authentically is empowering. It reminds you that you are the captain of your own ship. You will be able to navigate life with intention, respond to challenges with courage, and create a future that reflects your values and dreams. There will always be obstacles, difficult people, and unexpected setbacks, but when you act from your center, you can face these experiences with strength and resilience. By acting authentically now, you're preparing for a life that is meaningful, joyful, and deeply satisfying.

Remember, your worth does not need to be derived from external approval. Your confidence grows when you listen to your inner voice, honor your values, and act in alignment with your true self. The more you practice this inward-guided approach, the more authentic you will become. This is your path to a life of freedom, empowerment, and true fulfillment—a life that is entirely and beautifully your own.

LIVING BY A
NEW PARADIGM

*I*n this book, I have encouraged you to turn
inward and become more principle-centered.
This may feel countercultural, but stepping outside of
the usual pressures is essential for becoming a strong,
confident teen. Earlier chapters explored the challenges
of having fluctuating centers—trying to base your identity on everyone else's expectations rather than your
own beliefs and values.

When we let our identity unite with our parents,
peers, school, or extracurriculars, we lose touch with
who we truly are. More than that, our self-worth will

become dependent on the opinions of others. This overdependence can erode our self-esteem, diminish confidence, and make it difficult to recognize our authentic selves.

Thus, by building our self-esteem from the inside out, we can create a foundation for confidence, resilience, and authenticity. This is because how we feel about ourselves influences how we'll act in real situations. Feelings of uncertainty or awkwardness often reflect low self-esteem. By learning to become more inward-directed rather than outward-guided, we can start to trust ourselves and navigate life with strength.

The good news is self-esteem can be nurtured, one choice and action at a time. Every decision we make either honors or undermines our sense of self. Acting in alignment with our values strengthens self-esteem, while consistently acting against them weakens it. Ultimately, building self-trust is central to our identity. But do we have the courage to act according to our principles, especially in challenging situations? How we respond to peer pressure, conflict, or criticism reveals how resilient we are and how important it is for us to act autonomously and with integrity.

To build inner strength, it's important to recognize the signs of low self-esteem: giving in to peer pressure, constantly seeking approval, acting arrogantly to hide insecurity, or comparing ourselves to others. Healthy self-esteem, on the other hand, is reflected in standing up for ourselves, trusting our judgment, pursuing goals, celebrating others' successes, and maintaining a positive outlook.

This new paradigm is about shifting from outward-directness to inward-guided living. Instead of relying on social approval or external validation, you learn to center yourself on your own values, beliefs, and desires. This shift is not about isolation—it is about self-knowledge, resilience, and emotional intelligence. By practicing inward-guided living during the teen years, you lay the foundation for a fulfilling, authentic adult life.

Naturally, the teen years are social. However, our lives don't have to be predominantly social. We also have to make time to reflect on what's most important, such as building healthy habits that will lead to a resilient and successful life that is lived with integrity. In other words, we need to carve out emotional space to reflect, renew, and grow. This is essential in a culture that is dominated by external pressures to conform. The more often we practice this inward-directed approach, the more empowered, resilient, and content you will become.

Thus, take some time to explore these habits and practices by revisiting this book often. Remember, you don't need anyone else's approval to be the best version of yourself. Your authentic self is your greatest source of strength, joy, and fulfillment.

Living by a new paradigm is about choosing to center your life on your own values, beliefs, and desires rather than on external expectations. It is about becoming more inward-directed instead of outward-guided. This requires that you learn to act from your authentic self rather than conforming to peer pressure, social media, or the opinions of others. This shift may feel countercultural, but it is essential for building strong self-esteem, confidence, and resilience.

The teen years are a critical time for discovering who you are. These years are filled with social activity, constant comparison, and external pressures, yet they also offer the perfect opportunity to explore your inner world. By carving out time for self-reflection, solitude, and renewal, you create the mental and emotional space to understand your true self. This inward focus allows you to identify your values, clarify your beliefs, and recognize the activities, friendships, and experiences that genuinely bring you joy.

Developing self-esteem from the inside out is the cornerstone of the new paradigm I'm proposing. Remember, your worth and confidence do not depend on popularity, grades, or approval from others. It grows from honoring your commitments, keeping promises to yourself, and acting consistently in accordance with your beliefs and values. Each time you stand up for yourself, resist peer pressure, or follow your own judgment, you cultivate a resilient sense of identity. Over time, these practices become habits, and authenticity becomes a natural way of living.

This new paradigm also teaches you to embrace solitude and self-discovery as powerful tools. Enjoying your own company, pursuing personal hobbies, and taking time for reflection are not signs of isolation— they are ways to deepen self-knowledge and recharge your inner resources. Solitude allows you to listen to your inner voice more clearly, make decisions with clarity, and approach life's challenges with confidence.

Living by this paradigm is not about perfection; it is about consistent effort and self-awareness. You'll face situations that challenge your beliefs, test your courage, or expose you to criticism. How you respond in these moments reveals the strength of your self-esteem and the depth of your authenticity. By practicing inward-guided living now, you prepare yourself for an adult life that is empowered, fulfilling, and true to who you are.

Ultimately, embracing this new paradigm is about the freedom to be yourself, trust yourself, and live a life aligned with your values. The more you practice turning inward, reflecting on your beliefs, and acting authentically, the stronger and more confident you will become. Your life will no longer be dictated by external expectations but guided by the wisdom and integrity that come from knowing yourself deeply. This is the essence of living authentically, and it is the path to resilience, fulfillment, and lasting self-esteem.

CONCLUSION

Living Authentically and Empowered

As we reach the end of this book, it's important to step back and recognize the journey you have undertaken. You have explored habits that shape character, self-esteem, and authenticity. You have learned to be proactive rather than reactive, constantly renew and evolve, be a go-getter, determine your beliefs and values, develop autonomy through boundaries, and live courageously and authentically. Each of these habits, though challenging to practice, is a building block toward a life of purpose, resilience, and fulfillment.

At the heart of all these lessons lies a central principle: Your life belongs to you. The sooner you embrace this truth, the more empowered you will become. Many teens, and even adults, fall into the trap of living according to others' expectations. Whether it is from parents, friends, teachers, or society at large, there is constant pressure to conform, be someone you are not, or achieve success defined by external standards. This book has encouraged you to resist that external pressure and turn inward instead, cultivating self-awareness, self-trust, and self-love. By doing so, you'll begin to live from the inside out rather than the outside in.

The first step toward empowerment is **proactivity**. By taking responsibility for your actions and decisions, you become the author of your own story. Reactivity, which is allowing circumstances or others to dictate your behavior, usually leads to confusion, regret, and a loss of control. By being proactive, you reclaim your power and develop a sense of ownership over your life. This proactive stance supports every other habit in the book.

Constant renewal and evolution are the second cornerstone. Growth does not happen automatically.

It requires intentional effort, self-reflection, and the courage to leave behind habits, beliefs, and patterns that no longer serve you. Life is dynamic, and your mindset must be dynamic as well. Each day offers an opportunity to become a better version of yourself—more self-aware, more compassionate, more resilient.

Being a **go-getter** emphasizes the importance of initiative and perseverance. Complaining or waiting for circumstances to change will not produce results. True success comes from consistent action and a positive outlook, even when challenges arise. Taking initiative in your own life strengthens confidence, builds competence, and fosters self-respect.

Equally vital is the development of **beliefs and values**. Knowing who you are at your core is crucially important. What you stand for, what you believe in, and what you value—is foundational to authentic living. Without this clarity, it is easy to drift with the crowd and lose sight of what truly matters. By identifying your beliefs and values early, you create a compass to guide your decisions and actions, protecting your self-esteem from being shaped by fleeting opinions or peer pressure.

Autonomy through boundaries is closely connected. Once you understand your values, it is essential to act in alignment with them and establish boundaries that safeguard your energy, identity, and emotional well-being. Healthy boundaries are a sign of self-respect and self-trust. They allow you to engage meaningfully with others without compromising your authenticity.

Central to all of this is **authenticity**. Being authentic is not merely about honesty; it is about courage, self-love, and living in alignment with your deepest truths. Authenticity requires listening to your inner voice, trusting your intuition, and making choices that honor your values and passions. It means celebrating what makes your eyes sparkle, even if others do not understand it. The path of authenticity is often challenging, but it is deeply rewarding.

Building **self-esteem** from the inside out is an essential companion to authenticity. When your self-worth is based on external approval, it becomes fragile and easily shaken. By cultivating self-trust, keeping promises to yourself, reflecting on your beliefs, and nurturing your own growth, you create a resilient inner foundation. This self-esteem allows you to navigate life's challenges with confidence, resist peer pressure, and make choices that reflect your true self.

Living by this **new paradigm,** one of inward-guided living, self-reflection, and intentional choice, is ultimately about freedom. It is freedom from the need for constant validation, freedom from conformity, and freedom from fear of judgment. It is the ability to chart your own course, learn from mistakes without losing self-respect, and pursue a life of purpose and joy. Carving out time for reflection, solitude, and self-renewal empowers you to connect with your values, passions, and goals.

This paradigm also emphasizes resilience. Life will always present obstacles, challenging people, and unexpected setbacks. The difference lies in how you respond. When you act from your center, guided by your beliefs and values, you are equipped to handle adversity with confidence and composure. You become the captain of your own ship, navigating turbulence with clarity and strength.

As you move forward, remember that this is a life-long practice. Proactivity, renewal, self-knowledge, authenticity, self-esteem, and autonomy are not destinations. They are actually ongoing habits that require attention, courage, and reflection. Each day provides an opportunity to practice these habits, refine your values, and act in alignment with your true self. By consistently turning inward, you cultivate emotional intelligence, resilience, and a deep sense of fulfillment that no external circumstance can shake.

Ultimately, the message of this book is simple but profound: **You are the architect of your own life.** By living authentically, nurturing your self-esteem, and acting according to your deepest values, you create a life of empowerment, joy, and meaning. No one else can define your worth or dictate your path. Your choices, actions, and mindset shape the life you will lead. Embrace this responsibility with courage, self-love, and determination. The habits you have learned here are not just for your teen years—they are for your entire life. By practicing them faithfully, you will emerge as a confident, authentic, and empowered individual, capable of creating a future that reflects your truest self.

This is your life, your journey, and your opportunity. Live it authentically, act with courage, and honor the incredible potential that you have within you, because your adult years will be much more successful because of all the healthy habits that you developed through your teen years.

Perhaps instead of always partying, you can choose to take a more intentional approach. You can take the time to instead get to know yourself and create healthy habits that'll result in a healthy, happy, and fulfilled life. You earned it by all your hard work.

If you take the time to implement the eight habits I discussed at length in this book, I promise you will live a much more successful life, one where you're in the driver's seat of your life. What a feeling that is. Your confidence will grow, and you will live a life that's resilient, autonomous, and filled with integrity.

I am so proud of you for taking this important step of reading this book. You will also be glad that you did as you embark on your adult years with purpose and in the driver's seat of your life.

To a successful and beautiful life!

With Love!
Irene S. Roth

Taking Action

Integrating the 8 Habits for an Authentic Life

*N*ow that you have explored the eight habits, self-esteem, authenticity, and living by a new paradigm, it's time to take action. Knowledge alone is not enough. True growth happens when you intentionally practice these principles in your daily life. Think of this as your personal blueprint for living an authentic, confident, and empowered life.

1. **Daily Reflection:** Begin each day with a few minutes of self-reflection. Ask yourself: What values do I want to honor today? How can I act proactively rather than reactively?

Journaling is a powerful tool here—it helps you track your thoughts, clarify your beliefs, and reinforce your intentions.

2. **Set Small Goals:** Start with manageable actions that align with your values. Maybe it's speaking your truth in a conversation, asserting a boundary, or spending quiet time alone to listen to your inner voice. Each small step builds self-trust and strengthens your inner foundation.

3. **Practice Authenticity:** Look for moments where you can choose honesty over conformity. Speak up when it matters, pursue activities that bring you joy, and resist the urge to follow the crowd when it conflicts with who you truly are. Celebrate the unique qualities that make you, you.

4. **Build Resilience:** When faced with challenges or criticism, pause and act from your center. Reflect on your values before responding. Remember that setbacks are opportunities for growth, not measures of your worth.

5. **Renew and Recharge:** Prioritize time for yourself. Develop hobbies, enjoy solitude,

or create a personal retreat where you can reflect and recharge. This strengthens your ability to act from your center and maintain emotional balance.

6. **Review and Adjust:** On a weekly basis, revisit your habits, goals, and actions. Are they aligned with your values? Are you living authentically? Adjust where necessary. Growth is a continuous process, and self-awareness keeps you on the right path.

7. **Celebrate Progress:** Recognize every step you take toward becoming your authentic self. Growth is incremental, and celebrating your wins fuels motivation and confidence.

By putting these practices into action, you turn theory into experience, building a life that is deeply fulfilling and true to your essence. Each day becomes an opportunity to live authentically, nurture self-esteem, and embrace your power. This is your life—own it, shape it, and let it reflect the incredible person you are meant to be.

Summary of Path to Living Authentically

1. Habit #1: Be Proactive

Take responsibility for your choices; act from intention rather than reaction.

2. Habit #2: Constantly Renew and Evolve

Embrace growth; learn from mistakes; leave behind what no longer serves you.

3. Habit #3: Be a Go-Getter

Take initiative and act on your goals; small, consistent actions build momentum.

4. **Habit #4: Determine Your Beliefs and Values**

   Clarify what matters most; identify personal principles to guide decisions.

5. **Habit #5: Develop Autonomy Through Boundaries**

   Protect your energy; make decisions aligned with your values.

6. **Habit #6: Be Your Best**

   Strive for excellence in daily actions; cultivate personal discipline and integrity.

7. **Habit #7: Be Authentic**

   Express your true self; speak your truth; reject the need for external approval.

8. **Habit #8: Living Authentically and Building Self-Esteem**

   Trust your inner voice; make choices that reflect your values; nurture self-worth and confidence.

Final Stage: Living According to a New Paradigm

Integrate all habits into a cohesive lifestyle; live intentionally, authentically, and resiliently; navigate life from the inside out rather than the outside in.

RESOURCES

Habits & Personal Development

1. *Atomic Habits* by James Clear A guide to building good habits and breaking bad ones through small, incremental changes.

2. *The Power of Habit* by Charles Duhigg Explores the science behind habit formation and how habits can be changed.

3. *Tiny Habits* by BJ Fogg Focuses on creating habits by starting small and celebrating successes.

4. *The 7 Habits of Highly Effective People* by Stephen R. Covey A classic on personal effectiveness and leadership.

5. *The 7 Habits of Highly Effective Teens* by Sean Covey. Tailored for teens, this book adapts Covey's principles for a younger audience.

6. *Make Your Bed* by Admiral William H. McRaven Shares life lessons learned from Navy SEAL training.

7. *Deep Work* by Cal Newport. Advocates for focused work in a distracted world.

8. *Mindset* by Carol S. Dweck. Explores the concept of fixed versus growth mindsets.

9. *Grit* by Angela Duckworth. Discusses the power of passion and perseverance.

10. *The Compound Effect* by Darren Hardy Highlights how small, consistent actions lead to significant results.

Books About Teen Development & Self-Esteem

11. *The Self-Esteem Habit for Teens* by Lisa M. Schab Offers 50 simple ways for teens to build confidence daily.

12. *Be You, Only Better* by Kristi Hugstad. Focuses on self-care for young adults.

13. *Stop, Breathe, Chill* by Beth Stebner. Provides mindfulness exercises for teens.

14. *Express Yourself* by Emily Roberts. A guide to speaking up and being true to oneself.

15. *The Teen Girl's Anxiety Survival Guide* by Lucie Hemmen. Offers strategies to conquer anxiety.

16. *The Perfectionism Workbook for Teens* by Ann Marie Dobosz. Helps teens manage perfectionism.

17. *The Book of Self-Care* by Mary Beth Janssen. Provides remedies for healing mind, body, and soul.

18. *The Teen's Guide to World Domination* by Josh Shipp. Offers advice on self-confidence and success.

19. *You Are a Badass* by Jen Sincero. Encourages readers to embrace their inner power.

20. *Girl, Stop Apologizing* by Rachel Hollis. Empowers women to pursue their goals without guilt.

Books About Authenticity & Personal Growth

21. *Daring Greatly* by Brené Brown. Explores the power of vulnerability.

22. *Braving the Wilderness* by Brené Brown. Discusses the quest for true belonging.

23. *Radical Acceptance* by Tara Brach. Combines Buddhist teachings with psychology to promote self-acceptance.

24. *The Gifts of Imperfection* by Brené Brown. Encourages letting go of who you think you're supposed to be.

25. *Untamed* by Glennon Doyle. A memoir about embracing one's true self.

26. *The Four Agreements* by Don Miguel Ruiz. Offers a code of conduct based on ancient Toltec wisdom.

27. *The Art of Happiness* by Dalai Lama. Discusses the pursuit of happiness through inner peace.

28. *The Alchemist* by Paulo Coelho. A novel about following one's dreams.

29. *The Power of Now* by Eckhart Tolle. Focuses on living in the present moment.

30. *You Are Enough* by Mandy Hale. Encourages self-love and acceptance.

Books About Success & Leadership

31. *Start with Why* by Simon Sinek. Explores the importance of knowing your purpose.

32. *Leaders Eat Last* by Simon Sinek. Discusses leadership and organizational success.

33. *Drive* by Daniel H. Pink. Examines what motivates people.

34. *The Lean Startup* by Eric Ries. Focuses on innovation and entrepreneurship.

35. *Grit* by Angela Duckworth. Discusses the power of passion and perseverance.

36. *The 5 AM Club* by Robin Sharma. Advocates for waking up early to maximize productivity.

37. *Principles* by Ray Dalio. Shares life and work principles for success.

38. *The Magic of Thinking Big* by David J. Schwartz. Encourages thinking big to achieve success.

39. *The One Thing* by Gary Keller. Focuses on simplifying one's workload.

40. *How to Win Friends and Influence People* by Dale Carnegie. A classic on interpersonal skills.

Books About Teen-Focused Personal Development

41. *The Teen's Guide to World Domination* by Josh Shipp. Offers advice on self-confidence and success.

42. *Teenage Wisdom* by Josh Shipp. Provides insights and advice for teenagers.

43. *The 6 Most Important Decisions You'll Ever Make* by Sean Covey. Guides teens through critical life choices.

44. *The Teen's Guide to Social Media & Mobile Devices* by Jonathan McKee. Offers advice on navigating digital spaces.

45. *How to Be a High School Superstar* by Cal Newpor. Discusses achieving academic success without stress.

46. *The Teen's Guide to Personal Finance* by Joshua Holmberg. Introduces financial literacy for teens.

47. *The Teen's Guide to College & Career Planning* by Mark Rowh. Provides guidance on post-high school planning.

48. *The Teen's Guide to Money* by Jennifer L. Lane. Offers advice on managing finances.

49. *The Teen's Guide to Health & Wellness* by Sarah J. Mahoney. Focuses on physical and mental well-being.

50. *The Teen's Guide to Relationships* by Sarah J. Mahoney. Discusses building healthy relationships.

These books provide a diverse range of perspectives and tools to support teens in developing positive habits, building self-esteem, and embracing authenticity. Including them in your bibliography will offer readers a wealth of resources to further their personal growth journey.

REFLECTIVE QUESTIONS BASED ON THE 8 HABITS

Habit I: Be Proactive Instead of Reactive

1. How do I usually respond when things don't go my way?

2. Do I react impulsively or think before acting?

3. What situations trigger negative reactions in me?

4. How can I take responsibility for my actions more consistently?

5. When was a time I reacted instead of responding thoughtfully?

6. How would handling that situation differently have changed the outcome?

7. In what areas of my life can I be more proactive?

8. Do I let others' opinions dictate my choices?

9. How do I handle criticism?

10. What steps can I take today to act instead of react?

Habit 2: Constantly Renew and Evolve

11. What areas of my life feel stagnant?

12. How do I currently challenge myself to grow?

13. When was the last time I tried something new?

14. What new skills or habits do I want to develop?

15. How do I respond to failure or setbacks?

16. What is one change I can make today to improve myself?

17. Am I open to feedback from others?

18. How do I stay motivated to evolve as a person?

19. Do I set personal goals regularly?

20. How can I measure my growth over the next month?

Habit 3: Be a Go-Getter

21. What am I passionate about achieving?

22. How often do I take initiative in school or personal projects?

23. What goals do I have for the next year?

24. What prevents me from taking action toward my goals?

25. How do I handle challenges that feel overwhelming?

26. Am I persistent when I face obstacles?

27. How do I celebrate my accomplishments?

28. Who inspires me to take action and why?

29. How do I balance ambition with self-care?

30. What's one small step I can take today toward a bigger goal?

Habit 4: Determine Your Beliefs and Values

31. What values are most important to me?

32. How do my actions reflect my beliefs?

33. Do I compromise my values to fit in with others?

34. What would I do if my friends disagreed with my beliefs?

35. How often do I reflect on what I truly care about?

36. Which beliefs guide my decisions most strongly?

37. Do I act consistently with my values, even when it's hard?

38. How have my values changed over time?

39. What decisions have I made recently that reflect my values?

40. How can I make my daily actions align better with my beliefs?

Habit 5: Develop Autonomy Through Boundaries

41. How do I know when to say "no"?

42. Do I feel guilty when I set personal boundaries?

43. Which relationships respect my limits, and which don't?

44. How do I feel when I put my needs first?

45. How do I balance helping others with honoring my boundaries?

46. When have I allowed someone else's expectations to dictate my actions?

47. What is one boundary I can establish today?

48. How do I communicate my limits clearly?

49. Do I take responsibility for my own choices without blaming others?

50. How can I practice saying "no" without feeling guilty?

Habit 6: Be Your Best

51. What does being my best self mean to me?

52. How do I measure personal success?

53. Do I compare myself to others often?

54. When have I done something I'm proud of recently?

55. How do I stay motivated to improve?

56. What areas of my life could use more effort?

57. How do I celebrate progress rather than just results?

58. Who or what inspires me to strive for excellence?

59. Do I focus on strengths or weaknesses more often?

60. How can I challenge myself to grow this week?

Habit 7: Be Authentic

61. Do I feel comfortable being myself around others?

62. When do I feel like I'm pretending to be someone else?

63. How do I define my authentic self?

64. Do I listen to my heart when making decisions?

65. How do I respond to peer pressure?

66. Which parts of myself do I hide from others?

67. How can I show more of my true self each day?

68. Who supports my authenticity?

69. How do I feel when I act in alignment with my values?

70. What small action today can reflect my true self?

Habit 8: Live Authentically and Build Self-Esteem

71. How do I feel about myself right now?

72. What actions make me feel proud of who I am?

73. How do I handle failure or mistakes?

74. Do I rely on others for validation?

75. How do I practice self-love daily?

76. Which negative self-beliefs hold me back?

77. How do I protect my energy from negativity?

78. How do I celebrate my uniqueness?

79. Which habits strengthen my self-esteem?

80. How can I act with more confidence in challenging situations?

Integrative Questions Across All Habits

81. How do these habits connect with each other in my life?

82. Which habit do I struggle with the most? Why?

83. How do I feel when I practice all eight habits together?

84. What daily routines can I create to reinforce these habits?

85. How do my friendships influence these habits?

86. How can I turn setbacks into growth opportunities?

87. How do I remind myself to act from my values?

88. Which habit has the most positive impact on my self-esteem?

89. How do I balance self-improvement with enjoying life?

90. What does success mean to me beyond external approval?

Deep Reflective & Action-Oriented Questions

91. How would my life change if I fully embraced these eight habits?

92. What is one habit I want to master first, and why?

93. How can I track my progress in living these habits?

94. Which habits feel natural, and which require more effort?

95. How do I respond to criticism or failure while staying authentic?

96. How do these habits influence my decision-making?

97. Who can support me in developing these habits?

98. How do I stay consistent in practicing these habits during stressful times?

99. Which habit has already made a noticeable difference in my life?

100. How can I teach or inspire others to adopt these habits?

ACKNOWLEDGMENTS

*W*riting this book has been an incredible journey, and I am deeply grateful to everyone who helped bring it to life.

To the teens who inspired these pages—thank you for your honesty, courage, and curiosity. Your willingness to explore who you are and what matters most reminds me that authenticity is a lifelong journey worth taking. You are the heart of this book.

A special thank-you to my family and friends for your constant encouragement, patience, and belief in this project from the very beginning. Your support reminded me to keep showing up, even when the process felt challenging or uncertain.

To my mentors, teachers, and colleagues—thank you for modeling what it means to live with integrity and purpose. Your wisdom helped shape not just this book, but also my understanding of what it means to live authentically.

I am also deeply thankful to the readers, editors, and creative partners who offered thoughtful feedback, ideas, and enthusiasm along the way. Each insight helped this book grow into something more meaningful and practical.

Finally, to every reader who picks up this book—thank you for taking this step toward discovering your true self. May these words remind you that you are enough—right now, just as you are—and that you have the power to create a life that reflects your unique light. Never forget that your voice, dreams, and choices matter.

With gratitude and hope,
Irene S. Roth

LET'S CONNECT

Facebook: Irene Roth

Instagram: Irenesroth

X: @RothIrene

Email: Ireneroth218@gmail.com

MORE BOOKS BY
Irene S. Roth

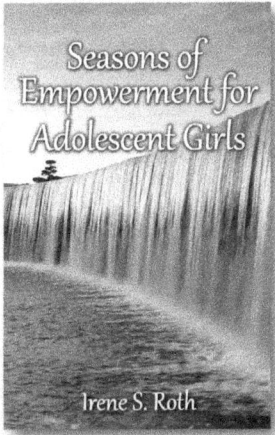

Seasons of Empowerment
for Adolescent Girls

ISBN: 978-1-61244-068-2

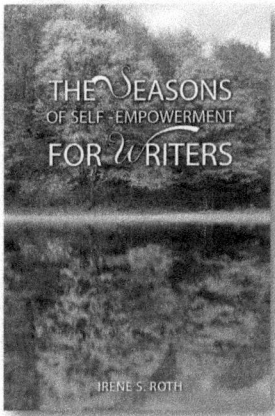

The Seasons of
Self-Empowerment for Writers

ISBN: 978-1-61244-054-5

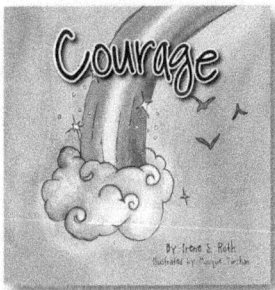

Courage

ISBN: 978-1-61244-068-2

KINDLE EDITIONS

The Materialist Teenager:
From Mindless Spending
to Mindful Consumption

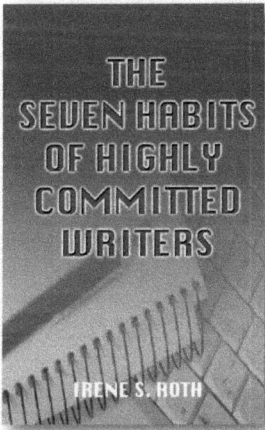

The Seven Habits of Highly
Committed Writers

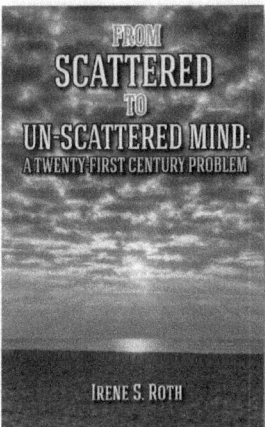

From Scattered to Un-Scattered
Mind: A Twenty-First
Century Problem

The Malaise of Technology

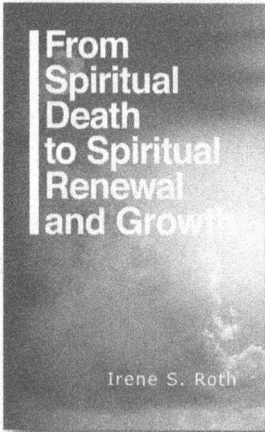

From Spiritual Death to Spiritual Renewal and Growth

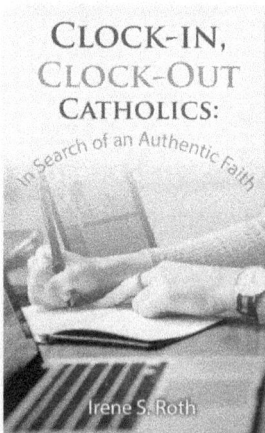

Clock-in, Clock-Out Catholics: In Search of an Authentic Faith

The Introverted Writer

The Excellent Writer

The Healthy Writer